MY DAILY "I GOT THIS" JOURNAL

A confident, powerful me—inside and out!

Ruth Wishengrad, M.Ed.

My Daily "I Got This" Journal
© 2025 UpBeats Media. All rights reserved.

All rights reserved. No part of this publication may be reproduced, stored in a retrieval system, or transmitted in any form or by any means—electronic, mechanical, photocopying, recording, or otherwise—without the prior written permission of the publisher, except in the case of brief quotations used in reviews or educational materials, with appropriate credit.

This journal is intended as a creative, educational resource to support emotional awareness, confidence, and well-being. It is not a substitute for professional advice, therapy, or mental health support.

Every effort has been made to ensure the content is accurate and helpful. However, the author and publisher make no guarantees and assume no responsibility for any actions taken by individuals based on the information provided. If you have concerns about a child's mental health or emotional well-being, please consult a qualified professional such as a healthcare provider, counselor, or school support staff.

This publication is provided with the understanding that the author and publisher are not engaged in rendering medical, psychological, or counseling services. If such expertise is needed, the services of a licensed professional should be sought.

For more resources and uplifting content, visit:
www.UpBeatsMedia.com

Printed in the United States of America
ISBN: 978-0-9966181-0-6

Cover & Interior Design by Ruth Wishengrad, M.Ed.
First Edition

This journal is dedicated to:

the little voice inside—the one that's powerful and strong and knows *you've got this* all day long!

🎶 **Want to hear the music behind the magic?**

Scan the QR code to enjoy your FREE song! Get ready to dance, sing, create—your way.

or visit: UpBeatsMedia.com/freesong

Welcome	6
Celebrate YOU!	9
Your CONFIDENT SUPERPOWERS!	19
The Moment is NOW!	29
There is only ONE YOU!	39
I Am the BEST I Can Be	49
FEELING the Way I FEEL	59
Taking a BREATH	69
Did you know you have SUPERPOWERS?	79

MY DAILY "I GOT THIS" JOURNAL

CONTENTS

What helps you BOUNCE back?	**89**
What made you SMILE today?	**99**
Finding the GOOD!	**109**
FEEL that POWER deep inside!	**119**
You Are LOVED (Always!)	**129**
Breathe in ... Breathe out ...	**139**
The ANSWER comes NATURALLY!	**149**
You Did It!	**159**
Certificate of YouGotThis-Ness!	**160**

Welcome to your very own 'I Got This!' Journal

Hi There!

I'm so glad you're here!

Guess what?

This journal is all about YOU—your feelings, your dreams, your superpowers, and all the amazing things that make you ... well, YOU!

Life can be full of all kinds of feelings—happy, excited, frustrated, or even sad, angry and lonely. And that's okay! This journal is a special space where you can write, draw, and explore those feelings while building your confidence and discovering just how awesome you really are!

It's not about being perfect—it's about being YOU, dreaming big, and celebrating all the things that make you the one and ONLY YOU!

Ready to get started?

You've got this - - -
Let's GO!

How to Use This Journal

Here's how it works:

1. **Take It One Page at a Time**
   There's no right or wrong way to use this journal. Start wherever you feel like and move at your own pace. You can write, draw, or just think about the questions—it's all up to you.

2. **Be Yourself**
   This journal is YOURS. Be as creative as you want. Use it to express your feelings, no matter what they are. Remember, all feelings are important.

3. **Dream Big and Have Fun**
   This is a place for big ideas, silly moments, and everything in between. Let your imagination run wild and don't hold back!

You can do this! - - -

4. **Come Back Anytime**
    Finished a page? Awesome! Want to come back later and add more? Go for it! This journal is here for you whenever you need it.

5. **Celebrate YOU**
    Every time you open this journal, you're doing something great for yourself. Give yourself a high five (or even a happy dance) for showing up and being YOU.

So choose your favorite pencil, pen, or markers, and let's go! Your big dreams and bold moves are waiting!

Ready, set, create! - - -

 Celebrate YOU!

Hippity Happy Birthday, to you, to you!

Whether today's your birthday or
it's just a regular ol' Tuesday,
it's time to celebrate YOU!

Discover what you love, dream big, and
throw a party for your awesome self.

Make wishes, giggle lots, and fill these pages
with sparkle, joy, and everything
that makes you... well, YOU.

 Hippity happy hippity happy YOU!

DAILY MORNING CHECK-IN

Sunday __/__/__	What is ONE thing you want to do today?
Monday __/__/__	What is ONE thing you want to do today?
Tuesday __/__/__	What is ONE thing you want to do today?
Wednesday __/__/__	What is ONE thing you want to do today?
Thursday __/__/__	What is ONE thing you want to do today?
Friday __/__/__	What is ONE thing you want to do today?
Saturday __/__/__	What is ONE thing you want to do today?

DAILY EVENING CHECK-IN

Sunday __/__/__	The BEST thing that happened today was:
Monday __/__/__	What is something you are looking forward to?
Tuesday __/__/__	Today I BELIEVED in myself when I . . .
Wednesday __/__/__	What KIND thing you did for someone today?
Thursday __/__/__	What is ONE thing that made you smile today?
Friday __/__/__	Today I was CONFIDENT when I . . .
Saturday __/__/__	The ONE thing I am most PROUD of today is:

All About Me
(Birthday Style!)

My name is
_____

My birthday is
_____

If I could plan the best birthday ever, I would
_____
_____
_____
_____
_____

My Memory Balloon

What's a memory that makes your heart do a happy dance?

I remember this moment because it made me feel

Smile - It's Your Birthday!!

Draw a picture of you on your birthday!

 # Birthday Treats

Draw a picture of all the treats you like to have on your birthday

My Favorite Things Song (Part 1)

Snuggly soft pillows and dancing in jammies,
Peach Jam and toast with my dog and Grammie,
Hopping in circles with glittery wings—
These are a few of my favorite things!

Now it's YOUR turn to write your own song of happy things!

- What's your favorite food? _____

- What always makes you laugh? _____

  _____

- What's the best feeling ever? _____

  _____

- What's something that makes you smile?

  _____

  _____

My Favorite Things Song (Part 2)

Draw or write your song!

My BEST Year Yet!

_____ years old

What are you most looking forward to this year?

_____

_____

_____

_____

_____

Your CONFIDENT SUPERPOWERS!

What *is* confidence, anyway?
It's that powerful feeling that helps you stand tall, smile big, and believe in yourself.

What helps *you* feel that way?
Maybe it's trying something new, doing something you love, or remembering a time you accomplished something amazing.

Take a moment to think about the things, people, or moments that fill you up with confidence—because those things are your *secret superpowers!*

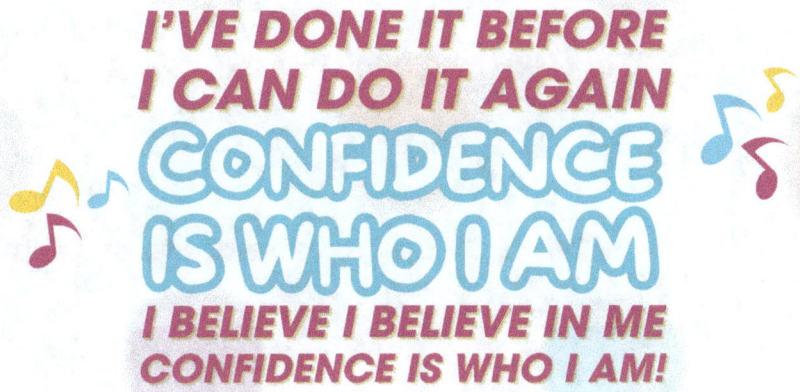

I'VE DONE IT BEFORE
I CAN DO IT AGAIN
CONFIDENCE IS WHO I AM
I BELIEVE I BELIEVE IN ME
CONFIDENCE IS WHO I AM!

DAILY MORNING CHECK-IN

Sunday __/__/__	**What is ONE thing you want to do today?**
Monday __/__/__	**What is ONE thing you want to do today?**
Tuesday __/__/__	**What is ONE thing you want to do today?**
Wednesday __/__/__	**What is ONE thing you want to do today?**
Thursday __/__/__	**What is ONE thing you want to do today?**
Friday __/__/__	**What is ONE thing you want to do today?**
Saturday __/__/__	**What is ONE thing you want to do today?**

DAILY EVENING CHECK-IN

Sunday __/__/__	The BEST thing that happened today was:
Monday __/__/__	What is something you are looking forward to?
Tuesday __/__/__	Today I BELIEVED in myself when I . . .
Wednesday __/__/__	What KIND thing you did for someone today?
Thursday __/__/__	What is ONE thing that made you smile today?
Friday __/__/__	Today I was CONFIDENT when I . . .
Saturday __/__/__	The ONE thing I am most PROUD of today is:

What are THREE things you can say to yourself to feel STRONG and CONFIDENT!

1.

2.

3.

Imagine you're a superhero. What are your powers?

_____

_____

_____

Draw yourself as a SUPERHERO!

What's one thing you've learned to do really well? How did you get good at it?

_____

_____

_____

What do you do when you're nervous about doing something new?

_____

_____

_____

_____

_____

My CONFIDENT CHEST

This is your CONFIDENT CHEST. It's a treasure chest, where you add your confident moments and memories.

If you could give advice to someone who feels shy, what would you say?

_____

_____

_____

When was a time you kept going even when things were hard? What did you do? How did you feel?

_____

_____

_____

_____

_____

CONFIDENT Moments and Memories

**Think about times you needed confidence ...
write or draw to explain those things.**

Doing something new for the first time.

Speaking in front of the class.

Saying "I don't know" or asking for help.

Apologizing when you make a mistake.

Speaking up about something you care about.

Helping a friend who's feeling sad or scared.

_____

_____

_____

_____

Build Your
CONFIDENCE LADDER

On each step, write something you're proud of doing, from small wins to big achievements.

 # The Moment is NOW!

Trying new things can be exciting... and sometimes kinda tricky. Sometimes your brain says, "I'm not sure I can do this!" And hey—that's totally normal!

That's when it's time to take a deep breath and say, **"I CAN DO IT!"** (Even if it takes a little practice.)

This part of your journal is all about believing in yourself, even when things get tough.

Let's explore ways to keep going, try again, and feel proud—because you're stronger than you think, and yep... *you've totally got this!*

DAILY MORNING CHECK-IN

Sunday __/__/__	**What is ONE thing you want to do today?**
Monday __/__/__	**What is ONE thing you want to do today?**
Tuesday __/__/__	**What is ONE thing you want to do today?**
Wednesday __/__/__	**What is ONE thing you want to do today?**
Thursday __/__/__	**What is ONE thing you want to do today?**
Friday __/__/__	**What is ONE thing you want to do today?**
Saturday __/__/__	**What is ONE thing you want to do today?**

DAILY EVENING CHECK-IN

Sunday ___/___/___	The BEST thing that happened today was:
Monday ___/___/___	What is something you are looking forward to?
Tuesday ___/___/___	Today I BELIEVED in myself when I . . .
Wednesday ___/___/___	What KIND thing you did for someone today?
Thursday ___/___/___	What is ONE thing that made you smile today?
Friday ___/___/___	Today I was CONFIDENT when I . . .
Saturday ___/___/___	The ONE thing I am most PROUD of today is:

THINGS I've LEARNED
(Even When They Felt Tricky!)

Some things feel hard at first...
and then—bam!—you get the hang of it!

Can you think of a few things that were tricky at the beginning, and then you figured them out?

Examples:
- I figured out how to tie my shoes.
- I learned to ride a bike without training wheels!
- I practiced writing my name—and now I'm a pro!

Write or draw 3 of them below!
What's something you're proud of learning?

Ooops! I made a MISTAKE!

Ever mess up? Yep–everyone does. Mistakes are part of learning and growing!

What didn't go the way you wanted?

_____

_____

What did you do after?

_____

_____

_____

_____

💬 Next time, say: "Oops! I'm still learning!" (Then give yourself a wink 😉 –because you've got this!)

 The SPECIAL POWER of the word YET!

Instead of saying, "I can't do it" ... add one special word YET. YET changes everything.

I can't do it... YET!" means you're still learning— and that's awesome.

Fill in the blank and see what happens!!

I can't __(ride my bike)__ YET. I'm working on it!

I haven't _____ YET, and I'm giving it a go!

I'm still learning to _____, and I get better every day!

I don't feel ready to _____ YET, and that's okay!

😊 I can't do _____ YET, and I'm learning a little more each day!

What are you working on?
Draw it or write about it below!!

From not YET to YES, I can!

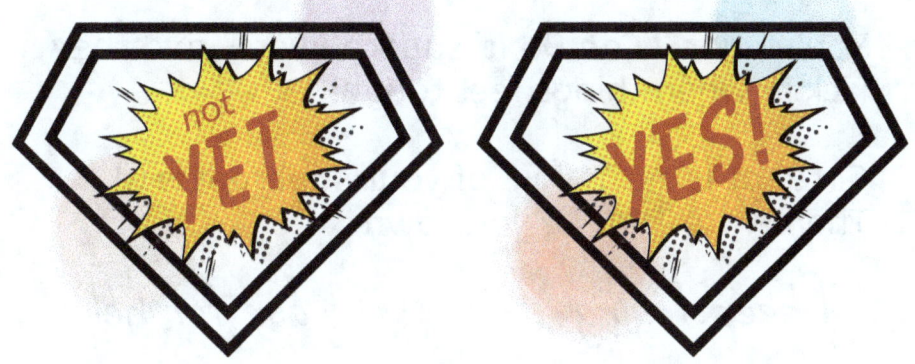

Write or draw 3 things you are working on changing from
not YET to .... YES, I did it!

My 'I Can Do It' Superpowers

You've got *'I Can Do It'* superpowers—and they kick in when things feel tough!

Circle at least THREE of your superpowers! Then write TWO of your own.

I keep trying   I ask for help

I take deep breaths   I say, "I got this!"

I learn from my mistakes

_____

_____

Draw yourself as a superhero showing off one of your awesome powers!

A NOTE to ME (from ME!)

Write a pep talk for yourself to read
when things feel tricky.

Example:

Hey [your name],

You're doing great. It's okay to go slow.

Take a breath and remember—you've got this!

✏ Add your special touch to make it extra YOU!

_____

_____

_____

_____

_____

My "I Did It!" Medal

You showed up. You kept going. You did it—woohoo! 🎉 Make yourself a medal that shines as bright as YOU.

Draw your own big, bold medal or trophy. Inside it, write or draw:

A moment I said, "I can do it!":
Now say it out loud:
"I can do it—and I DID!"

There is only ONE YOU!

Did you know you're one of a kind?
Really, It's true!

There is no one else in the whole wide world who thinks, feels, or dreams exactly like **YOU**.

Your kindness, your ideas, your laugh—everything that makes you *YOU*—is what makes you so special.

The world is brighter and better because you're in it!

I am fabulous
CONFIDENT
courageous
WONDERFUL
silly and happy

DAILY MORNING CHECK-IN

Sunday __/__/__	**What is ONE thing you want to do today?**
Monday __/__/__	**What is ONE thing you want to do today?**
Tuesday __/__/__	**What is ONE thing you want to do today?**
Wednesday __/__/__	**What is ONE thing you want to do today?**
Thursday __/__/__	**What is ONE thing you want to do today?**
Friday __/__/__	**What is ONE thing you want to do today?**
Saturday __/__/__	**What is ONE thing you want to do today?**

DAILY EVENING CHECK-IN

Sunday __/__/__	The BEST thing that happened today was:
Monday __/__/__	What is something you are looking forward to?
Tuesday __/__/__	Today I BELIEVED in myself when I . . .
Wednesday __/__/__	What KIND thing you did for someone today?
Thursday __/__/__	What is ONE thing that made you smile today?
Friday __/__/__	Today I was CONFIDENT when I . . .
Saturday __/__/__	The ONE thing I am most PROUD of today is:

Who are YOU?

What's your name?

_____

Do you know why your parents chose that name? Is there a story about your name?

_____

_____

_____

_____

_____

_____

Add the words that describe you, to the border around the picture frame.

Then, draw yourself inside!

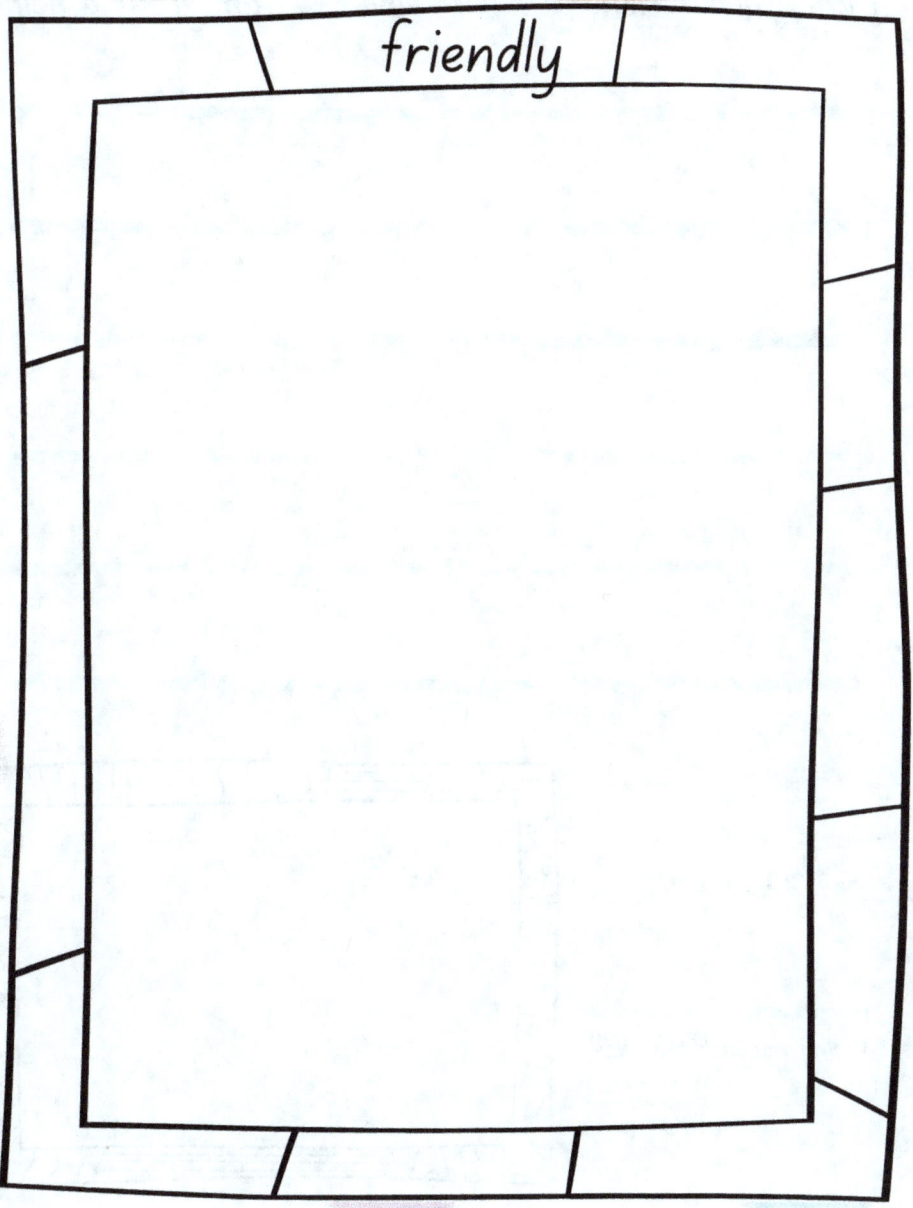

friendly

What makes you UNIQUE?

Write about what makes you special.
I am a good friend... I am kind... I am great a helper

_____

_____

_____

_____

_____

_____

this is me
_____
(being my SUPER-ME!)

What makes you YOU?

Circle the words that describe YOU!

funny
creative
smart
nice
kind
quiet
brave
loud
friendly
calm
curious
caring
helpful
adventurous
clever
shy
awesome
cool
thoughtful
energetic
strong
happy
confident
silly

What are your INTERESTS?

What are you good at? What do you like to do?

I'm good at sports . . . I love to read . . . I'm great at drawing

_____

_____

_____

_____

_____

_____

this is me

_____
(showing what I'm good at)

When do you feel the HAPPIEST being YOU?

riding my bike . . . cuddling with my dog . . . making things

_____

_____

_____

_____

_____

_____

me in my happy place

_____
(doing my 'happy dance!')

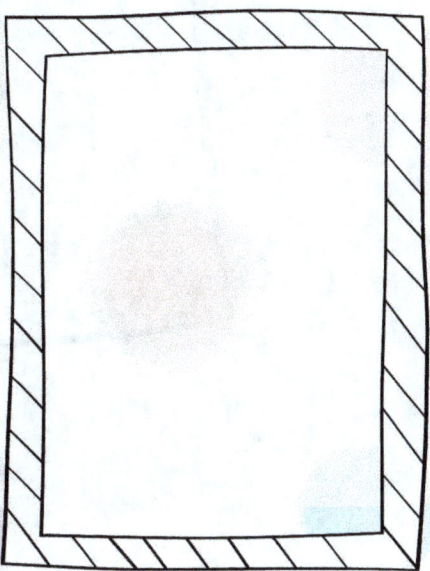

Create your SuperME T-shirt!

I Am the BEST I Can Be

You know what's really cool?

Being beautiful isn't just about how you look —it's about **who you are** on the inside, too!

Your kindness, your big ideas, and the way you care about others all make you shine.

And on the outside, your smile, your awesome style, and even the way you move show your unique sparkle to the world.

Let's take a moment to celebrate all the things that make you amazing—**inside and out!**

DAILY MORNING CHECK-IN

Sunday __/__/__	**What is ONE thing you want to do today?**
Monday __/__/__	**What is ONE thing you want to do today?**
Tuesday __/__/__	**What is ONE thing you want to do today?**
Wednesday __/__/__	**What is ONE thing you want to do today?**
Thursday __/__/__	**What is ONE thing you want to do today?**
Friday __/__/__	**What is ONE thing you want to do today?**
Saturday __/__/__	**What is ONE thing you want to do today?**

DAILY EVENING CHECK-IN

Sunday __/__/__	The BEST thing that happened today was:
Monday __/__/__	What is something you are looking forward to?
Tuesday __/__/__	Today I BELIEVED in myself when I . . .
Wednesday __/__/__	What KIND thing you did for someone today?
Thursday __/__/__	What is ONE thing that made you smile today?
Friday __/__/__	Today I was CONFIDENT when I . . .
Saturday __/__/__	The ONE thing I am most PROUD of today is:

ALL ABOUT ME
INSIDE and OUT!

What are things you love about yourself on the inside (like kindness, creativity)?

What are things you love about you on the outside (like your smile or hair)?

Imagine you are shining like a star...

What makes your light shine bright and sparkle—from the inside out?

Write about when someone said something nice about your personality. How did it make you feel?

_____

_____

_____

How do you show kindness to others?
Write about a time you made someone smile.

_____

_____

_____

_____

_____

COMPLIMENT Collage

Let's celebrate everything that makes you *amazingly YOU!*

Collect kind words, doodles, or things you love about yourself—and turn them into a bright, bold burst of *you-ness!*

Show off your sparkle, inside and out!

What is one thing that makes you feel CONFIDENT on the outside?

_____

_____

_____

_____

What is one thing that makes you feel STRONG on the inside?

_____

_____

_____

_____

MIRROR ME!

Imagine looking into a magical mirror—it shows everything amazing about you, inside and out!

What do you see? Your smile, your big heart, your kindness. Draw it. Write it. Show your sparkle!

Heart of Gold

Inside the heart, write or draw what makes you kind, caring, or helpful to others. It could be the way you listen, share, or cheer someone up with a smile!

FEELING the Way I FEEL

Sometimes we feel big feelings.
Excited. Sad. Frustrated. Giggly. Mad. *And* ...
sometimes we don't even know *what* we're feeling!

Using your words is one of your superpowers.
It helps people understand what's going on inside
your heart and your head.

Let's explore kind, clear ways
to say what you feel—and feel what you say!

I'll take a deep breath and count to ten...

DAILY MORNING CHECK-IN

Sunday __/__/__	**What is ONE thing you want to do today?**
Monday __/__/__	**What is ONE thing you want to do today?**
Tuesday __/__/__	**What is ONE thing you want to do today?**
Wednesday __/__/__	**What is ONE thing you want to do today?**
Thursday __/__/__	**What is ONE thing you want to do today?**
Friday __/__/__	**What is ONE thing you want to do today?**
Saturday __/__/__	**What is ONE thing you want to do today?**

DAILY EVENING CHECK-IN

Sunday __/__/__	**The BEST thing that happened today was:**
Monday __/__/__	**What is something you are looking forward to?**
Tuesday __/__/__	**Today I BELIEVED in myself when I . . .**
Wednesday __/__/__	**What KIND thing you did for someone today?**
Thursday __/__/__	**What is ONE thing that made you smile today?**
Friday __/__/__	**Today I was CONFIDENT when I . . .**
Saturday __/__/__	**The ONE thing I am most PROUD of today is:**

Whatcha THINKING?

What Helps Me FEEL BETTER

Everyone needs tools to feel better when things feel hard. Pick from the list below—or come up with your own!

- count to 10 slowly
- take balloon breaths
- talk to my grown-up

- cuddle my stuffed animal
- draw a picture
- cry (tears are okay!)

- giggle with a friend
- spin in a circle
- laugh at my own jokes

- take big belly breaths
- go to my quiet place
- stomp my feet

When I feel mad, I can _____.

When I feel sad, I like to _____.

When I feel worried, I can _____.

When I feel silly, I might _____.

When I feel happy, I want to _____.

✨ You're learning what works best for YOU! ✨

 # Name that FEELING

What does your face look like when you feel each feeling? Draw it your way!

○ happy   sad ○

○ mad   nervous ○

○ excited   tired ○

○ confused   proud ○

Say It Like This

Instead of yelling or stomping, you can use your words! Let's find kind ways to share your feelings

I feel ____loved____ when ____my cousin____ _giggles at my goofy dance moves._____.

Examples:
- I feel <u>left out</u> when <u>I don't get picked</u>.
- I feel <u>proud</u> when <u>I finish my drawing</u>.
- I feel <u>mad</u> when <u>someone takes my toy</u>.

✏️ Write 2 of your own:

I feel _____ when _____

_____.

I feel _____ when _____

_____.

Word Power!

Let's make a list of strong, clear feeling words you can use anytime.

Circle the ones you've felt before. Add your own too!

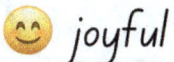 joyful    tired    annoyed

 frustrated    disappointed    silly

 nervous    loved   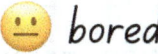 bored

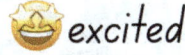 excited    confident    calm

Pick one feeling and draw what it looks like for YOU.

I Tell You What I Feel ...

I feel frustrated when...

I feel happy when...

I feel proud when...

I feel nervous when...

Right now, I feel

Taking a BREATH

Sometimes things are TOO MUCH—
Too loud, too busy, or too many feelings at once.

That's when it's time to stop.
Take a Time Out to take care of **YOU**.

When you slow down, your heart, brain,
and body all get a moment to reset.

In this section, you'll listen to your feelings,
take deep breaths, and find what
helps you feel good again.

Let's practice using your *pause power*.

DAILY MORNING CHECK-IN

Sunday __/__/__	What is ONE thing you want to do today?
Monday __/__/__	What is ONE thing you want to do today?
Tuesday __/__/__	What is ONE thing you want to do today?
Wednesday __/__/__	What is ONE thing you want to do today?
Thursday __/__/__	What is ONE thing you want to do today?
Friday __/__/__	What is ONE thing you want to do today?
Saturday __/__/__	What is ONE thing you want to do today?

DAILY EVENING CHECK-IN

Sunday ___/___/___	The BEST thing that happened today was:
Monday ___/___/___	What is something you are looking forward to?
Tuesday ___/___/___	Today I BELIEVED in myself when I . . .
Wednesday ___/___/___	What KIND thing you did for someone today?
Thursday ___/___/___	What is ONE thing that made you smile today?
Friday ___/___/___	Today I was CONFIDENT when I . . .
Saturday ___/___/___	The ONE thing I am most PROUD of today is:

The Power of the PAUSE

Create a Pause Button Sign

Make a sign for your room, desk, or backpack to let people know that you are pressing pause for a little while. ✨

Decorate it with anything that feels peaceful. 🖍️

What Joy Looks Like to Me

What does your happy place look like?

Rainbow Breathing

When things feel loud or too much,
it's a good time to stop and check in
with yourself and take some deep breaths.

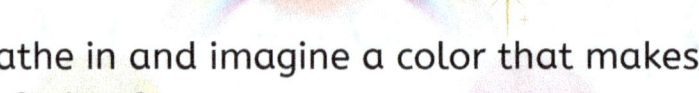

Breathe in and imagine a color that makes you feel safe.

Hold it for a second and feel it sparkle. Breathe out slowly and picture the color spreading all around you.

Do this with 3 different colors!

Draw your rainbow of calm!

Block Out the Noise

Does the world ever feel a little
too loud—even when no one's talking?
Too many thoughts ... too many feelings ...
Too much going on.
Let's make a quiet space that's just for YOU.

What colors do you see?
What's inside?

Inside my quiet space, I hear:
   ☐ Kind words   ☐ Just quiet
   ☐ Peaceful music   ☐ My calm thoughts

My Inner Calm

Write a story about how your brain and your heart get together to make you feel better.

_____

_____

_____

_____

Draw a picture of your brain & heart holding hands!

My Feel-Good Spinner

Decorate the spinner. Use it to help you reset your thoughts and feel good inside!

📎 Place a paperclip on the smiley face in the center with the tip of a pencil holding it down. Give it a spin!
Wherever it lands—do that thing!

Cloud Thoughts

Have you ever imagined floating on a big, fluffy cloud? It's like a hug, a break, and a giggle all rolled into one. Soft. Squishy. Full of feel-good feels.

Draw yourself on the cloud.

What's it like up there? What do you see, hear, or feel? Describe your cloud experience.

_____
_____
_____

Did you know you have SUPERPOWERS?

Positive thoughts are like tiny superheroes for your brain—they lift you up and remind you how amazing you are!

What do you love about yourself? Maybe it's your kindness, your courage, or how hard you try. On tough days, you can *grab* a positive thought—like *I'm strong* or *I can do hard things*—to help you feel better.

Keep those powerful thoughts 'in your pocket'— they're your *secret superpower!*

DAILY MORNING CHECK-IN

Sunday __/__/__	**What is ONE thing you want to do today?**
Monday __/__/__	**What is ONE thing you want to do today?**
Tuesday __/__/__	**What is ONE thing you want to do today?**
Wednesday __/__/__	**What is ONE thing you want to do today?**
Thursday __/__/__	**What is ONE thing you want to do today?**
Friday __/__/__	**What is ONE thing you want to do today?**
Saturday __/__/__	**What is ONE thing you want to do today?**

DAILY EVENING CHECK-IN

Sunday __/__/__	The BEST thing that happened today was:
Monday __/__/__	What is something you are looking forward to?
Tuesday __/__/__	Today I BELIEVED in myself when I . . .
Wednesday __/__/__	What KIND thing you did for someone today?
Thursday __/__/__	What is ONE thing that made you smile today?
Friday __/__/__	Today I was CONFIDENT when I . . .
Saturday __/__/__	The ONE thing I am most PROUD of today is:

Grab a BETTER thought!

Circle the sentences that make you feel good.

I can do hard things.

Mistakes help me learn and grow.

I am kind and thoughtful.

I am stronger than I think.

I have amazing ideas.

I am good at solving problems.

I am proud of myself for doing my best.

I can ask for help when I need it.

BETTER thoughts

Use some thoughts from the previous page, or create your own.
Write or draw good thoughts
to keep in your pocket when you need them.

What makes you feel proud of yourself?

___

Write about a time you were really brave.

Create a GRATITUDE poster.
Fill it with POSITIVE grateful THOUGHTS.

If your best friend were feeling sad, what would you say to cheer them up?

_____

_____

_____

What would you tell someone who feels nervous about trying something new?

_____

_____

_____

_____

_____

What are THREE nice things you've done for someone else?

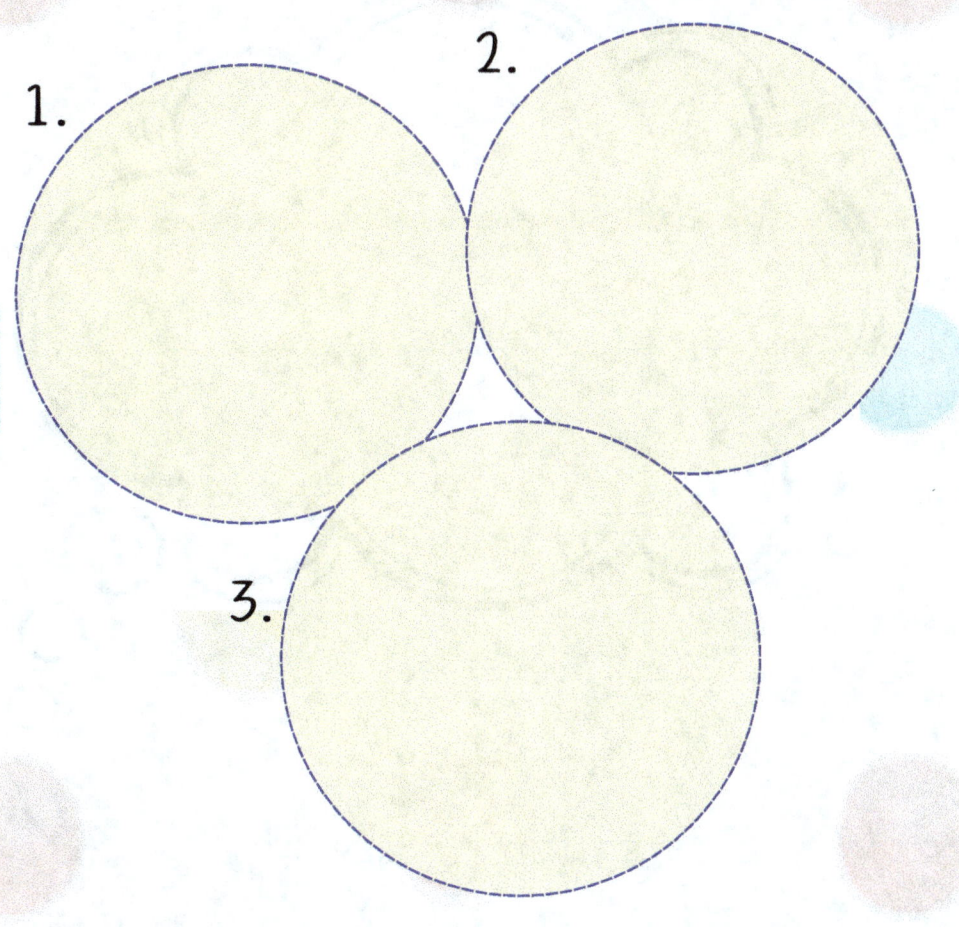

1.

2.

3.

What's a favorite memory that makes you SMILE?

What helps you BOUNCE back?

✨ Staying positive when things get tricky?
Yep—it's hard sometimes...
and *yes—it is* possible!

Even on tough days, you can look for the good—
even the teeny-tiny sparkly kind.

What can you do? ✨ Ask for help. ✨ Talk about your feelings. ✨ Remember—you've already made it through hard stuff before!

Every time you face a challenge with heart, you're building strength and showing yourself what's true: **You've got this. You really do.**

Say it out loud and proud: ***"I Got This!"*** 💪

DAILY MORNING CHECK-IN

Sunday __/__/__	**What is ONE thing you want to do today?**
Monday __/__/__	**What is ONE thing you want to do today?**
Tuesday __/__/__	**What is ONE thing you want to do today?**
Wednesday __/__/__	**What is ONE thing you want to do today?**
Thursday __/__/__	**What is ONE thing you want to do today?**
Friday __/__/__	**What is ONE thing you want to do today?**
Saturday __/__/__	**What is ONE thing you want to do today?**

DAILY EVENING CHECK-IN

Sunday __/__/__	The BEST thing that happened today was:
Monday __/__/__	What is something you are looking forward to?
Tuesday __/__/__	Today I BELIEVED in myself when I . . .
Wednesday __/__/__	What KIND thing you did for someone today?
Thursday __/__/__	What is ONE thing that made you smile today?
Friday __/__/__	Today I was CONFIDENT when I . . .
Saturday __/__/__	The ONE thing I am most PROUD of today is:

FEELINGS CHECK IN

☐ HAPPY   ☐ PEACEFUL   ☐ SCARED   ☐ SURPRISED   ☐ SAD
☐ ANGRY   ☐ CONFUSED   ☐ NERVOUS   ☐ CONFIDENT   ☐

THE FEELING IS:
☆ SMALL   ☆ MEDIUM   ☆ LARGE

I AM GRATEFUL FOR:

THE THOUGHTS IN MY HEAD

Ways to BOUNCE back!

Circle the sentences that would cheer you up.

Hugs make me feel better!

When I take a deep breath, it helps me feel calm so I can start again

A silly dance can make me laugh and forget what's bothering me!

Cuddling with animals (real or stuffed).

A favorite song makes me feel like dancing!

Fresh air and a little sunshine always make me feel better!

Tell myself, 'I am strong, and I got this!'

Think of a time when you felt sad or upset. What helped you feel better?

_____

_____

_____

If your friend was having a hard day, what would you say to help them feel better?

_____

_____

_____

_____

_____

Write or draw THREE things that make you smile, even on tough days.

Write about a superhero power you wish you had to help you when you're feeling down.

_____

_____

_____

_____

Draw yourself and your superhero power!

Write down THREE things you can say to yourself when you feel down. For example: "I've got this!" or "It's not great...yet!"

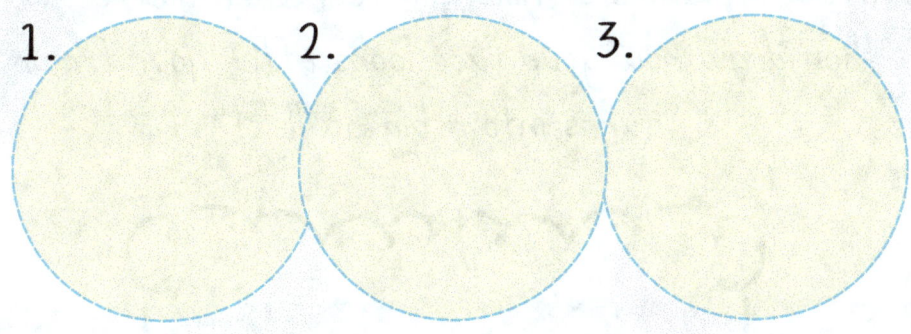

Draw a fun new dance move that makes you LAUGH! Give it a funny name like "The Smile Spinner" or "The Happy Hop!"

FLIP the FROWN
upside down ☺

Draw a picture of how you feel when you're sad, then draw how your face looks after your frown turns into a big SMILE!

What made you SMILE today?

Even on busy or bumpy days, there's always something that makes your heart do a happy dance. 😊

Maybe it's a kind word from a friend, a silly joke, or the sound of a bird singing outside. Even a tiny moment can bring a big smile!

What made *you smile* today?

Write it, draw it, or sing it out loud—and enjoy that happy feeling over and over again!

DAILY MORNING CHECK-IN

Sunday __/__/__	What is ONE thing you want to do today?
Monday __/__/__	What is ONE thing you want to do today?
Tuesday __/__/__	What is ONE thing you want to do today?
Wednesday __/__/__	What is ONE thing you want to do today?
Thursday __/__/__	What is ONE thing you want to do today?
Friday __/__/__	What is ONE thing you want to do today?
Saturday __/__/__	What is ONE thing you want to do today?

DAILY EVENING CHECK-IN

Sunday __/__/__	The BEST thing that happened today was:
Monday __/__/__	What is something you are looking forward to?
Tuesday __/__/__	Today I BELIEVED in myself when I . . .
Wednesday __/__/__	What KIND thing you did for someone today?
Thursday __/__/__	What is ONE thing that made you smile today?
Friday __/__/__	Today I was CONFIDENT when I . . .
Saturday __/__/__	The ONE thing I am most PROUD of today is:

Circle at least FIVE ways you can start your day with a SMILE!

laugh

dancing

sing

hug someone

giggle

stretching

drawing

deep breaths

yoga

listening to music

being grateful

pet snuggles

hug yourself

yummy breakfast

silly faces

What's a sound or smell that makes you smile?

_____
_____
_____

What's a kind thing someone did for you today?

_____
_____
_____
_____
_____
_____

Share the Joy

Write a letter or note to someone who made you smile today. Thank them for their kindness.

What's a compliment that you gave to someone today or this week?

_____

_____

_____

What's a nice thing you did for someone today?

_____

_____

_____

_____

_____

JOY Scavenger Hunt

Find FIVE things you can SEE, HEAR, or FEEL right now that make you happy!

My Happy List

A Joyful Memory

Write about a memory that always makes you smile. How does thinking about it make you feel?

_____

_____

_____

_____

_____

Draw a picture of your joyful memory.

my HAPPY thoughts

Finding the GOOD!

Every day has *something* worth smiling about!

Maybe it's a kind friend, your favorite snack, or the way the sunshine warms your face.

Noticing the good stuff helps you feel more joyful, more thankful, and more *you*.

What are you grateful for today? 💛
Draw it, write it, or make a list of all the little things that make your day brighter!

I SEE THE GOOD IN ME
I SEE THE GOOD IN YOU
I SEE THE GOOD IN US
ISN'T THAT . . .
MARVELOUS

DAILY MORNING CHECK-IN

Sunday __/__/__	**What is ONE thing you want to do today?**
Monday __/__/__	**What is ONE thing you want to do today?**
Tuesday __/__/__	**What is ONE thing you want to do today?**
Wednesday __/__/__	**What is ONE thing you want to do today?**
Thursday __/__/__	**What is ONE thing you want to do today?**
Friday __/__/__	**What is ONE thing you want to do today?**
Saturday __/__/__	**What is ONE thing you want to do today?**

DAILY EVENING CHECK-IN

Sunday __/__/__	The BEST thing that happened today was:
Monday __/__/__	What is something you are looking forward to?
Tuesday __/__/__	Today I BELIEVED in myself when I . . .
Wednesday __/__/__	What KIND thing you did for someone today?
Thursday __/__/__	What is ONE thing that made you smile today?
Friday __/__/__	Today I was CONFIDENT when I . . .
Saturday __/__/__	The ONE thing I am most PROUD of today is:

SEEING the GOOD in YOU!!

What are THREE things you love about yourself?

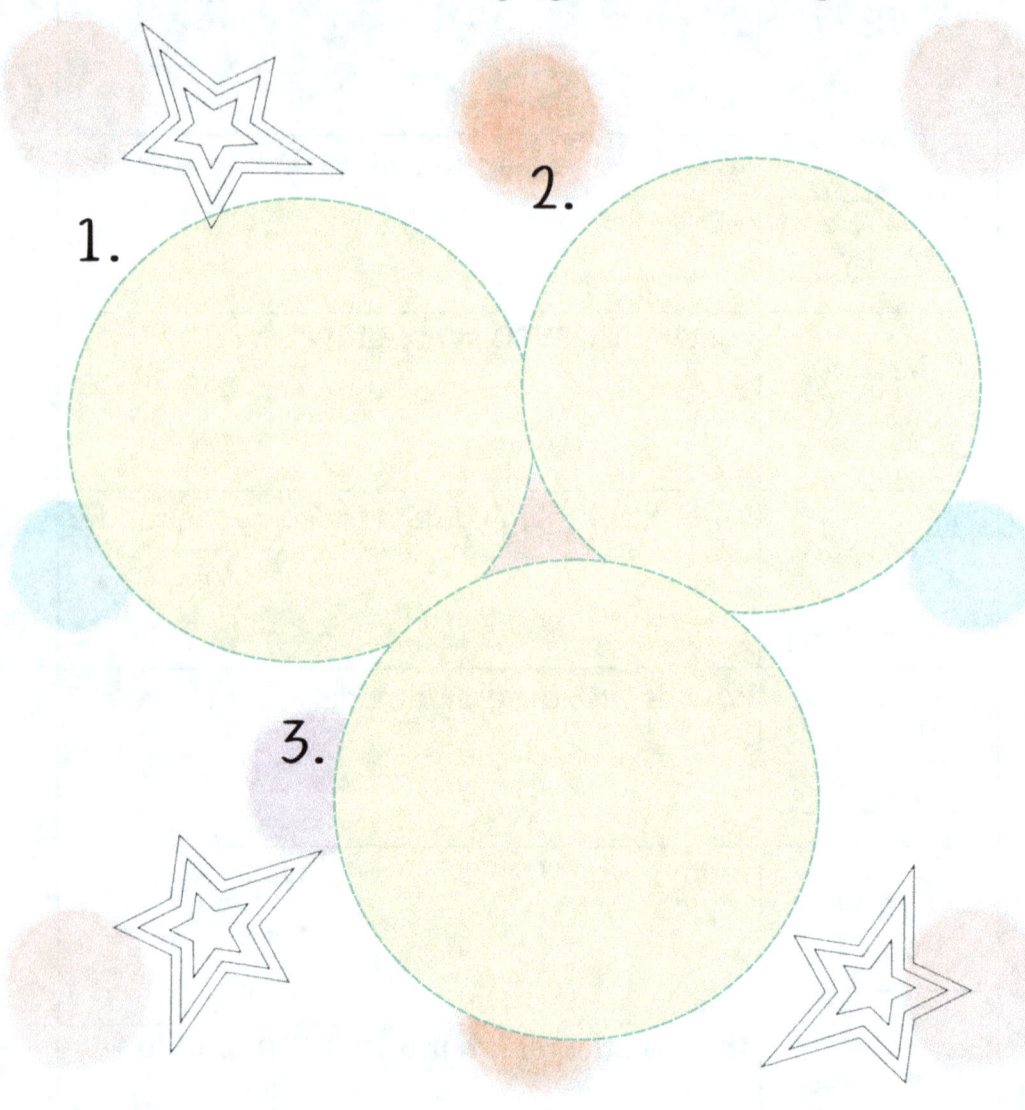

1.

2.

3.

SEEING the GOOD in OTHERS

Write about a time someone did something kind for you. How did it make you feel?

_____

_____

_____

_____

_____

_____

SEEING the GOOD in US

How does it feel when you and your friends or family help each other?

_____

_____

_____

_____

_____

_____

THINKING About the GOOD

How does thinking about good things make you feel inside?

_____

_____

_____

What's one good thing that happened today?

_____

_____

_____

Lifting Up and Shining Bright

What makes you feel like you're shining for the world to see?

_____

_____

_____

_____

_____

Marvelous Moments Collage

Make a collage of your "marvelous moments." Cut out pictures from magazines, draw, or write down the times when you saw good in yourself or others.

Kindness High-Fives

Trace your hand and write one kind word or good thing about yourself on each finger.

Then, write good things about friends or family in the spaces between.

FEEL that POWER deep inside!

When things feel hard and you're not sure what to do, there's *always something* that can help you keep going.

Maybe it's singing a happy song, taking a deep breath, or trying one little step at a time.

Tap into the beat of your heart—it's *always* there to help you move forward, stay strong, and keep trying.

Let's find what helps *you* keep *your beat!*

DAILY MORNING CHECK-IN

Sunday __/__/__	What is ONE thing you want to do today?
Monday __/__/__	What is ONE thing you want to do today?
Tuesday __/__/__	What is ONE thing you want to do today?
Wednesday __/__/__	What is ONE thing you want to do today?
Thursday __/__/__	What is ONE thing you want to do today?
Friday __/__/__	What is ONE thing you want to do today?
Saturday __/__/__	What is ONE thing you want to do today?

DAILY EVENING CHECK-IN

Sunday __/__/__	The BEST thing that happened today was:
Monday __/__/__	What is something you are looking forward to?
Tuesday __/__/__	Today I BELIEVED in myself when I . . .
Wednesday __/__/__	What KIND thing you did for someone today?
Thursday __/__/__	What is ONE thing that made you smile today?
Friday __/__/__	Today I was CONFIDENT when I . . .
Saturday __/__/__	The ONE thing I am most PROUD of today is:

What makes you feel like you sparkle and glow?

_____

_____

_____

What does it mean to you to "keep the beat" when things get tough?

_____

_____

_____

_____

_____

SPARKLE and GLOW Picture

Draw a picture of you to show how you SPARKLE and GLOW! Add words from the previous page to your drawing of UNIQUELY and SPARKLY you!

What is one thing that makes you feel STRONG and POWERFUL inside?

_____

_____

How do you stay positive and keep moving forward when something feels tricky or hard?

_____

_____

_____

_____

_____

THUMPITY THUMP Moments

Trace your hand on the page.

On each finger, write a moment when you kept going, even when it was hard.

In the palm, write how it felt to keep the beat and not give up.

Your SPARKLE and GLOW

Circle words that describe what makes you original and amazing. Write some of your own, too!

helpful   curious   caring

adventurous

energetic   thoughtful

_____

_____

_____

_____

_____

My POWER SONG

My CONFIDENCE BEAT

What keeps you going when things get tricky?

On each part of the drum, write one thing that helps you keep your beat—like asking for help, taking a break, or cheering yourself on with a power phrase like "I got this!"

You Are LOVED (Always!)

You don't have to be extra smiley to be loved.
You don't have to do anything perfect or fancy.
You are already lovable—just the way you are.

Even when you feel grumpy, tired, quiet, silly,
excited, or all the things at once...

You still matter. You're still YOU.
And that's pretty amazing!

This part is all about celebrating the real you—
the *one-of-a-kind, lovable, laugh-out-loud,
sometimes-needs-a-hug* YOU.

Let's enjoy all your feelings, faces,
and fabulousness. Because you're
already awesome... **just the way you are**.

DAILY MORNING CHECK-IN

Sunday __/__/__	What is ONE thing you want to do today?
Monday __/__/__	What is ONE thing you want to do today?
Tuesday __/__/__	What is ONE thing you want to do today?
Wednesday __/__/__	What is ONE thing you want to do today?
Thursday __/__/__	What is ONE thing you want to do today?
Friday __/__/__	What is ONE thing you want to do today?
Saturday __/__/__	What is ONE thing you want to do today?

DAILY EVENING CHECK-IN

Sunday __/__/__	The BEST thing that happened today was:
Monday __/__/__	What is something you are looking forward to?
Tuesday __/__/__	Today I BELIEVED in myself when I . . .
Wednesday __/__/__	What KIND thing you did for someone today?
Thursday __/__/__	What is ONE thing that made you smile today?
Friday __/__/__	Today I was CONFIDENT when I . . .
Saturday __/__/__	The ONE thing I am most PROUD of today is:

Celebrate YOU!
the Quirky, Cool, and One-of-a-Kind YOU!

Let's make a checklist of your *awesomeness*:

- ☑ I laugh in my own silly way

- ☑ I ask big questions

- ☑ I love to _____

- ☑ I care a lot about _____

- ☑ I'm not afraid to _____

- ☑ I feel proud when _____

Add your own and decorate with wild colors!

- ☑ _____

- ☑ _____

I'm ME – And That's AWESOME!

Let's make a list of what makes you... YOU!

I'm really good at _____

I always laugh when _____

People like my _____

I feel happiest when _____

Draw a picture of AWESOME, FABULOUS <u>YOU</u>!

My Many FACES

Draw 4 fun versions of YOU:

😊 Happy Me	😯 Surprised Me
😴 Sleepy Me	😛 Super-Silly Me

"All these faces are part of ME"

My Elephant Moment

Sometimes big feelings feel really heavy, like there's an elephant is sitting right on your chest! Let's help that elephant get hungry and move along!

Draw your elephant:
Make it as silly, colorful, or sleepy as you want.
Maybe it's wearing a tutu or holding a balloon!

When I feel like an elephant is sitting on me, I can...

☐ Take a deep breath
☐ Hug my stuffie
☐ Stretch like a giraffe
☐ Turn on some music
☐ Think of something that makes me giggle

Remember ...
"I'll find the peanuts, you just breathe."

What else helps me feel lighter? _____

_____

Smile! I love you!

Draw the faces or places
that make your heart do a happy dance!

Pillow Time!

Sometimes feelings get super big—and that's okay.
Yep—they happen! And it's okay to let them out.

Draw your favorite pillow—or make one up!
 zzZ Is it fluffy? Shiny? Covered in stars?
 zzZ What color is it when it's helping you feel calm?

Let it out!
When I feel _____, I might:
- ☐ Hug my pillow tight
- ☐ Yell into my pillow (go for it!)
- ☐ Cry and snuggle

Even when I'm feeling _____,

I am still safe. My pillow and I got this.

My "I AM LOVABLE" Puzzle

Draw four things that make you wonderfully lovable—just the way you are!

Breathe in ... Breathe out ...

Ahhh... sometimes you just need a moment to breathe, pause, and feel good again.
After a busy day or a big emotion, it helps to know what works *for you*.

Maybe it's stretching, deep belly breaths, listening to soft music, or imagining you're floating like a feather in space.

Everyone's reset button is a little different. This part of your journal is for you to breathe, reset, and feel good—inside and out.

✨ Get ready to recharge your sparkle.

DAILY MORNING CHECK-IN

Sunday __/__/__	What is ONE thing you want to do today?
Monday __/__/__	What is ONE thing you want to do today?
Tuesday __/__/__	What is ONE thing you want to do today?
Wednesday __/__/__	What is ONE thing you want to do today?
Thursday __/__/__	What is ONE thing you want to do today?
Friday __/__/__	What is ONE thing you want to do today?
Saturday __/__/__	What is ONE thing you want to do today?

DAILY EVENING CHECK-IN

Sunday __/__/__	The BEST thing that happened today was:
Monday __/__/__	What is something you are looking forward to?
Tuesday __/__/__	Today I BELIEVED in myself when I . . .
Wednesday __/__/__	What KIND thing you did for someone today?
Thursday __/__/__	What is ONE thing that made you smile today?
Friday __/__/__	Today I was CONFIDENT when I . . .
Saturday __/__/__	The ONE thing I am most PROUD of today is:

Floating FEATHER Meditation

What helps you feel floaty, relaxed, or just "ahhh... better"?

Maybe it's deep breathing, reading a book, hugging a friend, or listening to music.

Draw more feathers and label them with the things that help you feel light and good inside.

A soft and sparkly moment, just for you. ✨

What's your BEST?

What are THREE things that feel like the BEST in your life right now?

_____

_____

_____

_____

_____

Draw a picture of one of those BEST things!

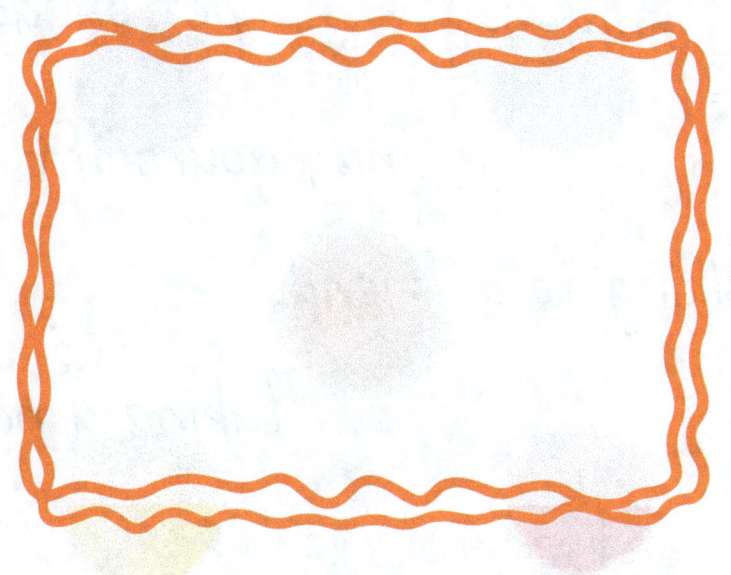

RELAXATION checklist

Circle the things that will help you relax.

hug someone

singing

deep breaths

stretching

drawing

yoga

resting under a blanket

humming

pet snuggles

hug yourself

talking to a friend

taking a nap

What colors make you feel relaxed? Why?

_____

_____

_____

Draw a picture with those colors ... how does your picture make you feel?

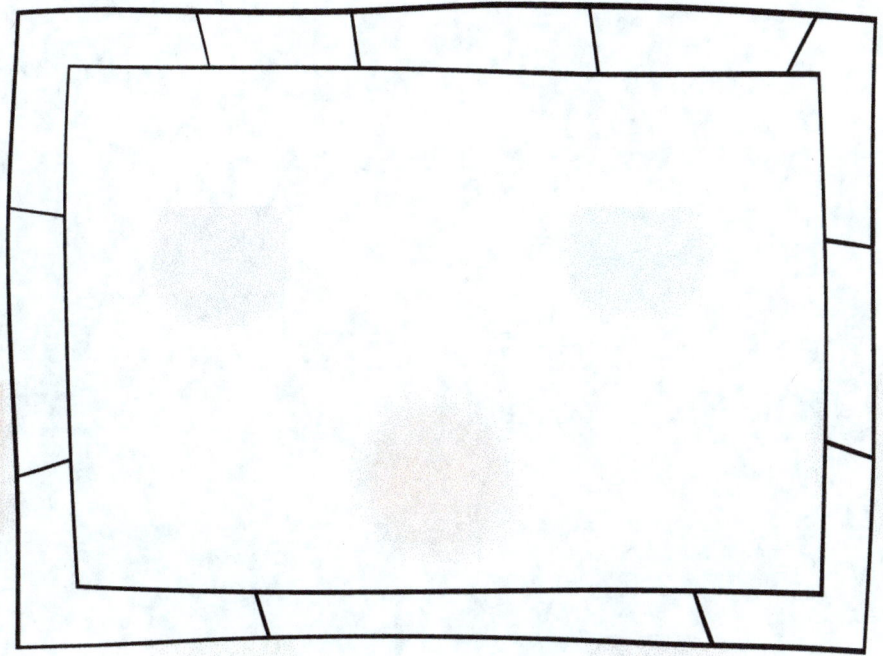

Bubble Breaths

Instructions:
Pretend you're holding a bubble wand.
Breathe in through your nose... Then breathe out
slowly through your mouth to *blow* a giant bubble.

Draw something that helps you feel good,
for example, a happy thought
or something you are proud of.

What makes you feel relaxed?

_____

_____

_____

Write a story about a time you were super relaxed. Who were you with? What were you doing?

_____

_____

_____

_____

_____

THIS IS MY HAPPY PLACE

The ANSWER comes NATURALLY!

Sometimes not knowing can feel a little tricky... or even frustrating. Guess what? That's totally okay!

Not knowing the answer doesn't mean you're stuck— it means you're about to learn something new.

You can pause, take a breath, ask questions, look for clues, or try again. Every time you wonder, explore, and keep going—you're growing stronger and smarter.

So, remember:
Not knowing isn't the end...
It's the beginning of discovering something new!

DAILY MORNING CHECK-IN

Sunday __/__/__	What is ONE thing you want to do today?
Monday __/__/__	What is ONE thing you want to do today?
Tuesday __/__/__	What is ONE thing you want to do today?
Wednesday __/__/__	What is ONE thing you want to do today?
Thursday __/__/__	What is ONE thing you want to do today?
Friday __/__/__	What is ONE thing you want to do today?
Saturday __/__/__	What is ONE thing you want to do today?

DAILY EVENING CHECK-IN

Sunday __/__/__	The BEST thing that happened today was:
Monday __/__/__	What is something you are looking forward to?
Tuesday __/__/__	Today I BELIEVED in myself when I . . .
Wednesday __/__/__	What KIND thing you did for someone today?
Thursday __/__/__	What is ONE thing that made you smile today?
Friday __/__/__	Today I was CONFIDENT when I . . .
Saturday __/__/__	The ONE thing I am most PROUD of today is:

FEELINGS CHECK IN

- ☐ HAPPY
- ☐ PEACEFUL
- ☐ SCARED
- ☐ SURPRISED
- ☐ SAD
- ☐ ANGRY
- ☐ CONFUSED
- ☐ NERVOUS
- ☐ CONFIDENT
- ☐

THE FEELING IS: ☆ SMALL ☆ MEDIUM ☆ LARGE

I AM GRATEFUL FOR:

THE THOUGHTS IN MY HEAD

Big QUESTION Brainstorm

1. Write questions you have today—big or small.
2. Pick one question and write how you could start finding the answer.

The ANSWER Inside of ME

Write about a time when you found an answer all by yourself. How did it feel? Draw a picture of yourself feeling proud.

_____

_____

_____

_____

_____

QUESTION Detective

Pretend you're a detective looking for clues to a tricky question. Draw or write about what tools or ideas could help you solve it.

_____

_____

_____

_____

_____

MOVE and THINK

When you're stuck on a question, moving can help! Write down a fun way to take a break—like dancing, playing outside, or stretching. Then, try it the next time you're unsure of what to do.

What are things will you do when you are stuck and need to clear your mind?

_____

_____

_____

_____

_____

SOLUTIONS SUPERPOWER

Think about a question you need to solve.
Put on your "superpower solutions hat" . . .

Draw how you will solve the problem..

I've got the ANSWER!!

Question Jar

This is your "Question Jar".
Write down questions you're curious about and come back to them later. Get curious ... ask anything! Explore all kinds of things ... and you know ... the answers just may be inside of you ☺

 # You Did It!

You've sparkled, dreamed, and imagined—and made this journal your very own.

Now it's time to **celebrate** everything you've felt, learned, and discovered.

Get ready for your very own official *"I Got This!" Certificate* on the next page!

Decorate it. Display it. And then ... it's **Happy Dance Time!**

CERTIFICATE OF YouGotThis-ness

This is to celebrate

_____

for finishing the "I Got This!" Journal and being awesome and sparkle-filled!

You laughed, felt, created, and showed up as **YOU**---
and that deserves
a big ol'
WooHoo!

Signed with sparkle by: Date:

Ruth
_____   _____

Keep shining, keep smiling, and remember: You've got this - and you always will!

www.ingramcontent.com/pod-product-compliance
Lightning Source LLC
Chambersburg PA
CBHW050341010526
44119CB00049B/648